WHAT IF I OWNED
EVERYTHING?

Lauree and L. Allen Burkett are the founders of **Money Matters for Kids**™. Their vision is to help children and teens understand the biblical principles of *Stewardship God's Way,* and they are developing fun and innovative materials, products, and programs to meet that need. Be sure to look for the **Money Matters for Kids**™ *Teaching kids to manage God's gifts* emblem of quality on children's and teens stewardship products. We welcome your comments and suggestions. Contact us by writing to:

Money Matters for Kids™
Lynden, Washington 98264-9760

Lightwave Publishing is a recognized leader in developing quality resources that encourage, assist, and equip parents to build Christian faith in their families.

Under the direction of Rick Osborne, Lightwave has been producing high quality materials since 1984.

Lightwave Publishing also has a fun kid's Web site and an internet-based newsletter called *Tips & Tools for Spiritual Parenting.* This newsletter helps parents with issues such as answering their children's questions, helping make church more exciting, teaching children how to pray, and much more. For more information, visit Lightwave's Web site at www.lightwavepublishing.com or write to:

Lightwave Publishing, Inc.
133
800–5th Avenue, Suite 101
Seattle, WA 98104-3191

Lightwave Publishing, Inc.
Box 160
Maple Ridge, B.C.
Canada   V2X 7G1

What If I Owned Everything?

Copyright © 1997 by Lauree and L. Allen Burkett for text and illustrations. All rights reserved. Written permission must be secured from the publisher to use or reproduce any part of this book, except for brief quotations in critical reviews or articles.

Published in Nashville, Tennessee, by Tommy Nelson™, a division of Thomas Nelson, Inc.

Scripture quotations are from the *International Children's Bible, New Century Version,* © 1986, 1988 by Word Publishing.

Tommy Nelson:
Managing Editor: Laura Minchew
Project Editor: Beverly Phillips

Lightwave:
Project Director: Rick Osborne
Art Director: Terry Van Roon
Project Editor: Christie Bowler
Assistant Illustrator: Ken Save

Cover Design: Anderson•Thomas Design, Inc.
Cover Illustration: Chris Kielesinski

Library of Congress Cataloging-in-Publication Data

Burkett, Larry

What if I owned everything? / by Larry Burkett; with Lauree Burkett.

p. cm.

Summary: A brother and sister try to outdo each other imagining who has the most or biggest or best, until they realize that everything they have comes from God.

ISBN 0-8499-1509-0

[1. Competition (Psychology)—Fiction. 2. Brothers and sisters—Fiction. 3. Christian life—Fiction.]
I. Burkett, Lauree.   II.Kielesinski, Chris, ill.   III. Title.

P27.B9228Wh   1997

[E]—dc21   97-24438
                                                                 CIP
                                                                  AC

Printed in Mexico

97 98 99 00 01 02 03 RRD 9 8 7 6 5 4 3 2 1

WHAT IF I OWNED
EVERYTHING?

LARRY BURKETT
with Lauree Burkett
Illustrations by Chris Kielesinski

Tommy
NELSON

Thomas Nelson, Inc.

Nashville

Especially for Parents
A LETTER FROM LARRY

What If I Owned Everything? leads us to the important questions of life. Can things make me happy or bring me joy? Can things buy me friends to make me a nice person to be around? Most importantly, can things satisfy that most basic need God planted deep inside me to have a meaningful relationship with Him and His Son, Jesus Christ?

As I began teaching the biblical principles of handling finances in 1973, I recognized immediately how necessary it is to begin that training at an early age. When I started teaching, there was nothing available that taught these principles. Over the years we at Christian Financial Concepts have developed some materials to help parents teach their children but, in general, I have focused my teaching on adults, not children.

One of the things I learned a long time ago is that whatever I could talk people into, somebody else might come along behind me and talk them out of. But whatever I could share with them from God's Word, nobody would ever be able to talk them out of. And, I'm sure you are well aware that what children can discover and learn on their own will have a lasting impact on their lives.

Therefore, as my son and daughter-in-law venture out to begin providing you with materials focused on *teaching children stewardship God's way,* I am proud to introduce them to you and am thrilled to have had a part in this book. And, as with other projects we have done, it is always a privilege to work with our friends at Lightwave Publishing.

Allen's and Lauree's hearts' desire is to open children's eyes, and thereby their hearts, to the exciting truth that God owns everything. God loves us and cares for us and gives us all that we need to serve Him with our whole hearts. He wants us to manage our gifts well, using His wisdom, so we might prove to be good and faithful servants—or stewards—of what He gives us.

I pray that God will use this book to spark a desire in your children's hearts to know God, to be good stewards, to desire His best, and to walk in His ways all their lives. As you read this beautiful and entertaining book with your children, use it as a springboard to share these truths with them; then, watch them enjoy their own discovery of God's ownership in their lives.

God bless you!

Larry Burkett

Larry Burkett

"Give this command to those who are rich with things of this world. Tell them not to be proud. Tell them to hope in God, not their money. Money cannot be trusted, but God takes care of us richly. He gives us everything to enjoy. Tell the rich people to do good and to be rich in doing good deeds. Tell them to be happy to give and ready to share. By doing that, they will be saving a treasure for themselves in heaven. That treasure will be a strong foundation. Their future life can be built on that treasure. Then they will be able to have the life that is true life."

1 Timothy 6:17–19

That day will be remembered forever. The twins, Jenny and Jeremy, didn't plan on it being different. It just happened! The longest, most unbelievable Better-Than-Best Match-Off in all of history!

"Next time up I'm gonna hit a home run."

"Yeah? Well, I'm gonna hit the ball into tomorrow!"

"Well, I'm gonna knock it into next week!"

"Next year!"

"Next century!"

"Eternity!"

It could have ended there. But not this mighty record-breaking contest. It kept on until it seemed as if their imaginations would explode!

"Ten times more than anything you can ever say," Jeremy continued.

"Hey, we always end that way," answered Jenny. "Let's really use our imaginations!"

"All I can imagine right now is an enormous ice-cream cone. How much money do we have?"

They both searched their pockets. "Enough for one double and one single scoop," Jenny counted.

"I get the double," Jeremy exclaimed.

"No way! Besides the ice-cream truck doesn't come for hours."

"Let's have a contest," he suggested. "Whoever imagines the most gets the extra scoop."

The contest was on!

"I imagine a triple-dip waffle cone," shouted Jeremy, "with all the extras."

"An ice cream bigger than your head," Jenny replied. "Vanilla, rocky road, and caramel pecan smothered in chocolate sauce."

"Well, what if I had one as big as a car? Ten flavors, hot fudge sauce, rainbow sprinkles, and nuts."

"What if I had one as big as a house?! It would have a hundred flavors, buckets of sauce and sprinkles, mounds of whipped cream, and loads of cherries." Jenny laughed.

"I can beat that!" Jeremy stated.

He was right.

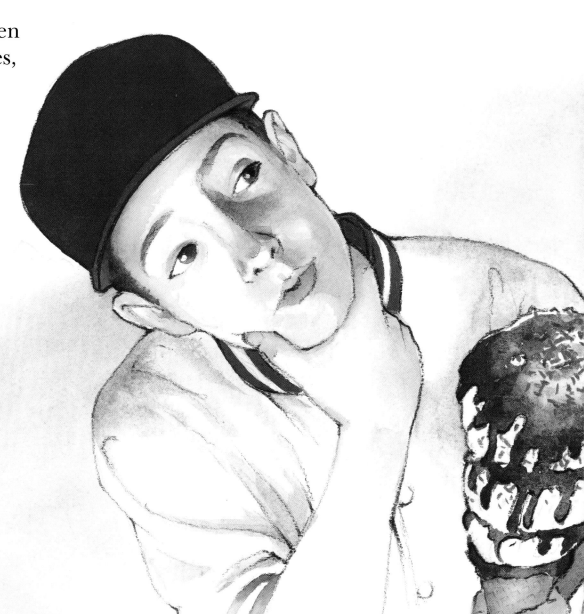

"What if I had all the ice cream in the world? Truckloads of sauce, nuts, and sprinkles. Mountains of whipped cream. Barrels of cherries. Ice cream forever!"

"You'd get sick!" Jenny told him. "It would melt and make a mess."

"Hey, who says it has to make sense?" Jeremy argued.

"Of course it has to make sense! Besides, that would be selfish. What would everyone else eat on a hot summer day?"

"I'd share. That would be even more fun!" Jeremy grinned, "I win."

"Sharing would be good. But you haven't won yet! Toys are even better than ice cream!"

13

"What if I had a life-size Molly-Does-It-All Doll? She could do everything."

"Well, what if I had a zillion building blocks?" asked Jeremy. "With all the special kits and motors and gadgets. I could build anything— a robot, planes, cities!"

"Oh, yeah! What if I got a new toy every day for a whole year . . . 365 birthdays."

Jeremy thought for a second. "A whole toy store!" he cried. "Just imagine . . . shelves and shelves of toys! Rows and rows of shelves of toys . . ."

"What if," Jenny exclaimed, "I owned every toy in the whole world?! All the dolls, all the blocks, every toy from every toy store . . ."

"Hey!" Jeremy interrupted, "Wait a minute! I can't own all the ice cream in the world, but you can own all the toys in the world? Besides, you already have tons of cool toys."

"Well, I don't want all the toys for myself. I'll make sure every kid everywhere has the best toys. And, I will give a toy to every kid on his birthday—and each kid can choose his own gift. I win!"

"Giving toys away would be cool," Jeremy said. "But everyone knows what you ride is better than what you play with!"

"What if I had an A-number-one, super-duper, 15-speed mountain bike?" he asked. "With mirrors, lights, a super-soft gel seat, and a water bottle built right in! The shiniest metallic blue and gold . . ."

"What if I had a really cool, razzle-dazzle, spin-on-a-dime, bright pink speed boat? With a canopy and white leather seats!" Jenny said.

"Well, what if I owned a candy apple red, top-of-the-line, computer-rigged, super-spy sports car?"

"Better yet!" proclaimed Jenny. "My very own supersonic jet! I could go to the World Series. I could see the world."

Jeremy jumped excitedly! "What if I owned the most radical, robotical, retro-rocket intergalactic spaceship?! I'd drink the Milky Way dry. I'd . . ."

"Oh, Jeremy, where would you park it?" Jenny interrupted. "Dad already has to keep reminding you to take care of your bike and put it away each night. How would you look after a spaceship?"

Jeremy knew she was right. He did need to take better care of his toys. But he wasn't about to give up yet. "Where you live is bigger than what you ride!"

"You're right!" Jenny agreed. "What if I had a three-story treehouse with a super-fantastical circular slide? I could slide right down into my very own pool. I'd have a lookout tower and a cookie-making machine. And a special room for my very own tea parties and sleepovers."

"Well, what if I owned a gigantic mansion? It would have huge rooms . . . big enough for an adventure-tube playground and trampolines and even a baseball field! And a swimming pool big enough for me and my pet whale! I'd have my own cook. Cookies and pies, hamburgers and fries. I'd . . ."

Jenny took her turn. "What if I owned a castle? Secret passages. Moats. Drawbridges. The tallest towers so I could see my whole kingdom!" She sighed dreamily, "Queen Jenny of ZazaZufendorzal and her zillion adoring subjects."

"Being Queen would be really hard. Just think how much time you'd need to spend caring for a zillion people. That's God's job!" Jeremy reminded her.

"Okay, I resign my throne. God can take care of the people. But He is so awesome, I'm sure He'd let me keep the castle. I win."

"Not yet! What if I . . ."

". . . owned everything we've said so far, plus . . ."

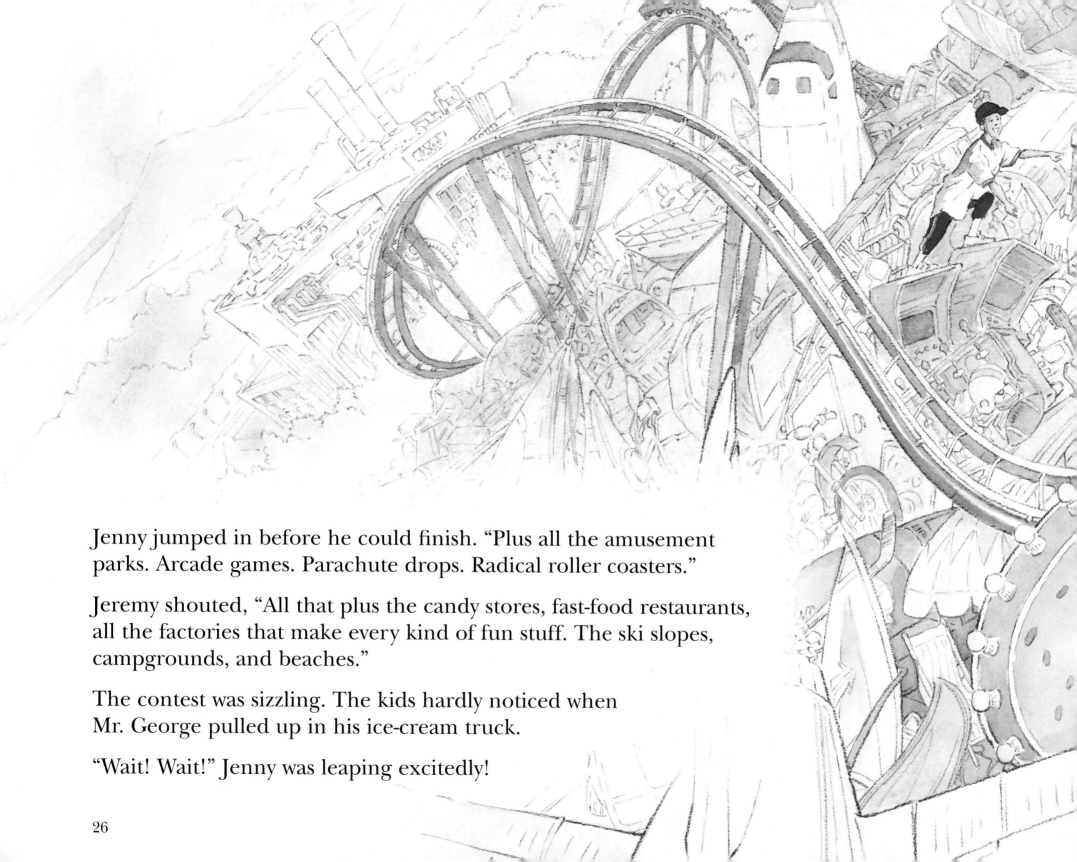

Jenny jumped in before he could finish. "Plus all the amusement parks. Arcade games. Parachute drops. Radical roller coasters."

Jeremy shouted, "All that plus the candy stores, fast-food restaurants, all the factories that make every kind of fun stuff. The ski slopes, campgrounds, and beaches."

The contest was sizzling. The kids hardly noticed when Mr. George pulled up in his ice-cream truck.

"Wait! Wait!" Jenny was leaping excitedly!

26

"What if I owned

EVERYTHING?"

"That's it! I win!" Jenny announced.

Mr. George didn't want to interrupt, so he just started scooping up the twins' favorite flavors.

But Jeremy wasn't giving up yet. "Hey, that would mean everyone else would have nothing!"

"I would make sure that everyone has everything they need whenever they need it," Jenny replied.

"How could you do that? You can't know everything and be everywhere all at once. Only God can do that!"

Jenny stopped and thought a second. She grinned, "Okay, Jeremy, you're right, only God can do that. And I'm really glad He's the one taking care of us!"

Jeremy added, "You know we can't own everything because it really belongs to God. But when we take care of the things He gives us and share with others, He can trust us with even more."

"Yeah, you're right, that's called being a good steward. And I think for remembering what's really important you get the double."

Mr. George smiled at the twins. "I tell you what, I'll give you both a double scoop. Enjoy!!"

"Really, Mr. George? Thanks!" The twins were smiling from ear to ear!

And that's how it happened . . . the biggest "Better-Than-Best Match-Off" ever! Well, at least for now . . .